CALCULUS

FOR KIDS

JOLPIC KIDZ

JOLPIC KIDZ

Calculus for Kids

First Published: April 2022

Jolpic Kidz is a publishing company of educational books written for kids.

For more info, mail us at jolpic@gmail.com

JOLPIC KIDZ

A gift for you

Enjoy your gift! From Bobby Hamrick

amazon Gift Receipt

Scan the QR code to learn more about your gift or start a return.

Calculus for Kids: Basic Concepts of Calculus for Beginners
Order ID: 113-4343622-7366650 Ordered on December 4, 2024

CONTENTS

NUMBERS

Why do we use numbers?

We generally use numbers to count things. Suppose, someone asked you the question,

How many books do you have in your bookshelf?

What will you do to answer it?
You should go to your bookshelf, and start counting the books uttering the numbers.

1, 2, 3, 4, 5, 6, 7...

When you finish your counting, you are able to tell the number of your books.

Numbers are not only useful to count things, but also to measure quantities.

If someone asks you the following questions,

What is the temperature today?

What is the distance of your school from your home?

What is your height?

What is your weight?

You have to use numbers to answer these questions. However, you have to mention measuring units along with the numbers.

Your answers are quite similar to the following:

- Todays temperature is 21 $^{\circ}$C.

- The distance of my school from my home is 3 kilometer.

- My height is 152 centimeter.

- My weight is 40 kilogram.

FRACTIONS

Sometimes fractions are used instead of whole numbers.

Imagine, you went to a restaurant and bought three pizzas.

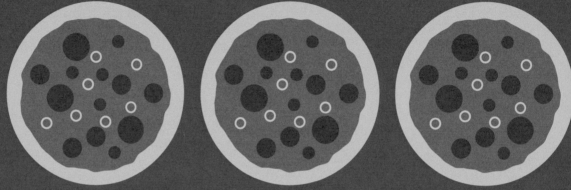

But you did not eat them all. You were able to eat two of them wholly, and a portion of the third one.

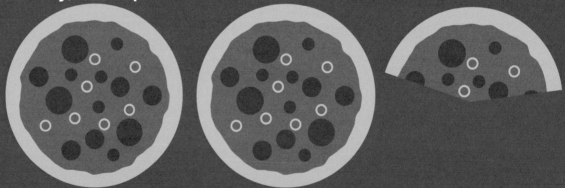

What is your answer if someone asks the question,

How many pizzas did you eat?

To calculate the number of pizzas that you ate, you need to understand the concept of fraction.

There is no problem to tell that you ate two pizzas wholly. Now for the third one, you have to divide the pizza into several equal segments.

In this case, your answer will not be a whole number, but a fraction.

Let's divide the pizza into 7 equal segments, and assume you ate 3 segments among them.

Total number of pizzas you ate,

$$1 + 1 + 3/7$$

$$= 2\frac{3}{7}$$

When we consider a part of a number rather than a whole number, we call that part a 'fraction'.

Fractions are frequently written in decimal forms. For example 1/2 can be written alternatively as 0.5.

Let's understand how 1/2 and 0.5 are the same.

$$\frac{1}{2}$$

The fraction, 1/2 has 1 in its numerator and 2 in its denominator. If we multiply any whole number with both of its numerator and denominator, the fraction does not change its value.

Let's multiply 5 with the numerator and the denominator of 1/2.

$$\frac{1}{2} = \frac{5}{10} = 0.5$$

If any number is divided by 10, 100, 1000, 10000 etc., only the decimal value is changed for that number keeping the digits unchanged. Decimal point will move one place to the left side for each 0.

Verify the following:

$$\frac{1}{5} = 0.2 \qquad \frac{1}{4} = 0.25 \qquad \frac{2}{5} = 0.4$$

$$\frac{3}{5} = 0.6 \qquad \frac{3}{4} = 0.75$$

Thousands Hundreds Tens Ones Tenths Hundredths Thousandths

1234.567
Decimal Point

Some numbers can not be exactly written in decimal forms.

For example if we try to write the following fractions in decimal forms, we get,

$$\frac{1}{3} = 0.3333333333...$$

$$\frac{2}{6} = 0.6666666666...$$

$$\frac{1}{7} = 0.14285714285...$$

In such cases, the numbers after decimal point will be repeated forever.

Rational and Irrational Numbers

There are some fractional numbers which can not be represented in P/Q forms (where P and Q are whole numbers. Those numbers are called Irrational numbers.

- For example, the ratio of circumference and diameter of a circle is an irrational number, and its value is,

3.14159265358979323846264338...

This number is known as π (pi) and its value is always the same for any circle.

- The square roots of most of the numbers are also irrational.
  For example,
  √2 = 1.41421356...
  √3 = 1.73205081...
  √5 = 2.23606798...
  √7 = 2.64575131...

For a rational fractional number, the digits after the decimal point are recurring. Whereas, for a irrational number the digits are not recurring.

We generally use these numbers to count things.

1, 2, 3, 4, 5, 6, 7, 8 ...

They are known as Natural Numbers.

Suppose there are some books on the table.

You can tell there are 4 books on the table by counting them.

But what would your answer be if the table was empty?

You should tell that there was 0 book on the table.

Thus 0 is the smallest whole number that we are able to use for counting physical objects.

In higher mathematics, the numbers which are less than 0 are often used.

$$-4, \ -3, \ -2, \ -1$$

They are known as negative numbers.

-5

A negative sign is written before any negative number.

If you ever say,

"There is -5 book on the table."

It sounds absurd because we can not count any physical thing using negative numbers.

Then what is the significance of negative numbers?

The Significance of Negative Numbers

We can understand the significance of negative numbers if we take the example of a thermometer.

We often use centigrade scale to measure temperature with a thermometer. This temperature scale is constructed taking melting and boiling point of water as standard. The melting point of water is marked as 0, and the boiling point of water is marked as 100, and this temperature range is divided into 100 units.

There is no problem if we want to measure any temperature which is greater than or equal to the melting point of water. We will get positive values in those cases. But what do we get the reading if we try to measure a temperature which is less than the melting point of water?

Obviously we get a negative reading on a thermometer.

You can verify the fact keeping a centigrade scale thermometer inside a freezer. A freezer always maintains a negative temperature, otherwise no ice would be frozen inside of it.

Number Line

We can construct a number line showing both positive and negative numbers on it. As we move to the right from 0 on the number line, we get positive numbers in increasing order. And if we move left from 0, we get negative numbers in decreasing order.

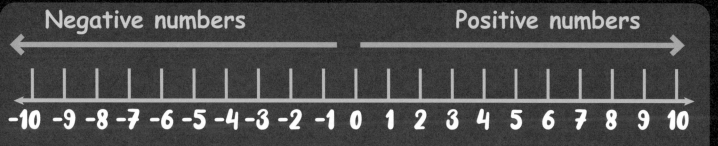

Apart from the temperature scale (or any other measuring scale which can show a negative value), negative numbers have other significances too in mathematics. However, we rarely use negative numbers in our real lives.

A few examples and their mathematical meanings

- "He moves -3 meter to the right."
  It actually means that he moves 3 meter to the left direction.

- "One of your friends takes -7 candies from you."
  It means your friend gives 7 candies to you.

A quantity may be a Variable or a Constant

If a quantity does not show a definite value always, the quantity may be considered as a variable.

For example, your height and weight do not show the same values every years. They change every year. If you measure your height and weight at this moment, you will get their values. But if you compare them to their values of the previous years or the upcoming years, you will notice the differences. So, you can say that your height and weight are variables with respect to years.

If a quantity does not change its value, the quantity is considered as a constant.

Now you think about the height of the Eiffel Tower and the weight of this book. Their height and weight do not change with time unless someone breaks the tower or tears the pages of this book. Thus you can say these two quantities are constants.

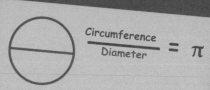

$$\frac{Circumference}{Diameter} = \pi$$

The ratio of the circumference of any circle to its diameter is also constant. This ratio is known as, π (pi).

Classify the following quantities as either constant or variable

- Total number of fingers in your hands and legs

- Time

- Number of playing cards in a whole deck

- The amount of water you drink everyday

Answers:

- You have 20 fingers in your hands and legs, and this number does not change. Thus it is a constant quantity.

- Time changes every moment, so time is a variable quantity.

- A whole deck of playing cards contains 52 cards, so it is a constant. If you take away a few cards from a deck, it does not remain a whole deck.

- The amount of water you drink everyday is a variable because you do not drink the same amount everyday.

In higher mathematics, variables and constants are often represented by alphabets and symbols instead of specific numbers.

Let's consider a rectangle of height 3 centimeter and width 5 centimeter.

To determine its area, you should multiply the height and the width.

$$3 \times 5 = 15$$

Thus 15 square centimeter is the area of the above rectangle.

If we want to determine the area of another rectangle of height 5 centimeter and width 8 centimeter, we should use the same technique.

Area is,

$$5 \times 8 = 40 \text{ square centimeter}$$

We should multiply the length and the width of any rectangle to determine its area.

$$\text{Area of a rectangle} = \text{Length} \times \text{Width}$$

Thus we can say that the height and the weight are two variables and their multiplication results the area of a rectangle of any size and shape. Now if we replace the numerical values of length and width with two alphabets L and W respectively, a generalized form may be shown,

$$\text{Area of a rectangle} = L \times W$$

Where L is the numerical value of length and W is the numerical value of width.

Similarly, the area of any circle can be represented as ,

$$\text{Area of a circle} = \pi r^2$$

Here π (circumference/diameter) is a constant and r is a variable representing the radius of any circle.

Now we are going to understand the concept of function with the help of different examples.

Imagine you have a brother who is 2 years younger than you.

Your age and your brother's age, both are variables as they increase by one every year. Thus we can replace them with two alphabets x and y respectively. Moreover, the age difference of you and your brother remains constant in every year.

Since your brother is 2 years younger than you, it is possible to determine your brother's age if you know your own age, and vice versa.

Your age is, x
Your brother's age is y

Since your brother is 2 years younger than you, alternatively you can write,

Your brother's age is, (x - 2)

$$y = x - 2$$

Thus it can be said that your brother's age is a function of your age.

Generally a function is written using the notation, f(x).

$$y = f(x)$$ [We replace the expression (x - 2) with f(x)]

The area of a rectangle is calculated multiplying two variables, its height and width. So we can tell that area of a rectangle is a function of its height and width.

$$Area\ of\ a\ rectangle = f(l,w)$$

Similarly the area of a circle is a function of its radius.

$$Area\ of\ a\ circle = f(r)$$

Function on a Cartesian Coordinate

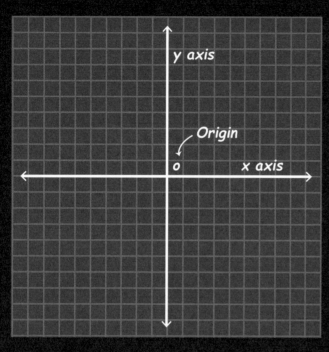

A Cartesian coordinate is a combination of two perpendicular intersecting straight lines. The vertical line is known as y axis, and the horizontal line is known as x axis. These two axes intersect at the origin.

These two axes represent two different variables. These two axes are divided into several units, and each unit represents the numerical value of those variables. The positive and the negative values of those variables are shown in the figure.

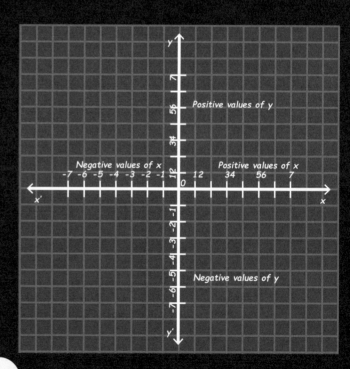

Now we are ready to plot the relation between your and your brother's age.

Your brother is 2 years younger than you. So the relation of two ages,

$$y = x - 2$$

Where x and y are your age and your brothers age respectively.

First we make table:

Your age	Your brother's age
When you were 0 year old	Your brother was not born.
When you were 1 year old	Your brother was not born
When you were 2 years old	Your brother was 0 year old (your brother was born)
When you were 3 years old	Your brother was 1 year old
When you were 4 years old	Your brother was 2 years old
When you were 5 years old	Your brother was 3 years old

Now we should put a few points on the coordinate representing your age and your brother's age, and connect those points with a straight line.

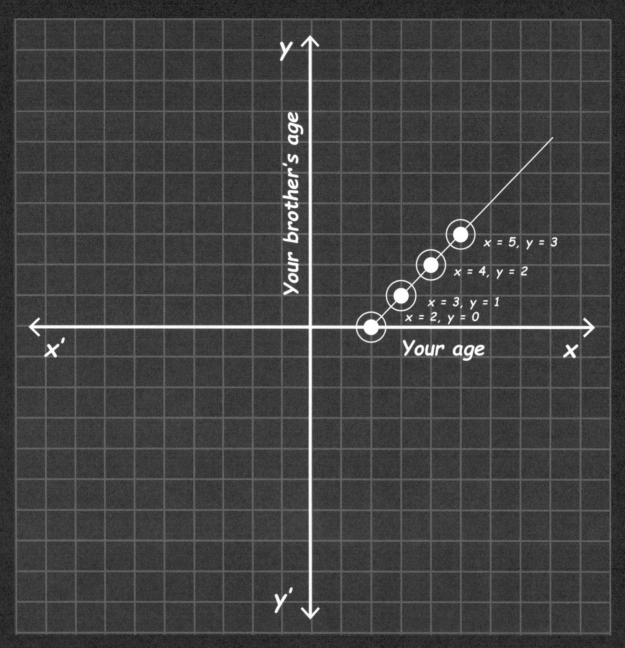

The values of x and y at every point on this straight line are representing the ages of you and your brother.

Another Example:

Imagine you have a friend who loves to eat bananas everyday. From the first day to seventh day in a given week, he eats number of bananas following the function (2x + 1), where x represents the day of that week. Draw a graph representing the number of bananas eaten by him with respect to the days of that week.

Let's consider he eats y bananas on x^{th} day.
As the function is already given, we can write,

$$y = 2x + 1$$

Corresponding Table:

Day (x)	Number of bananas (y)
1	2×1 + 1 = 3
2	2×2 + 1 = 5
3	2×3 + 1 = 7
4	2×4 + 1 = 9
5	2×5 + 1 = 11
6	2×6 + 1 = 13
7	2×7 + 1 = 15

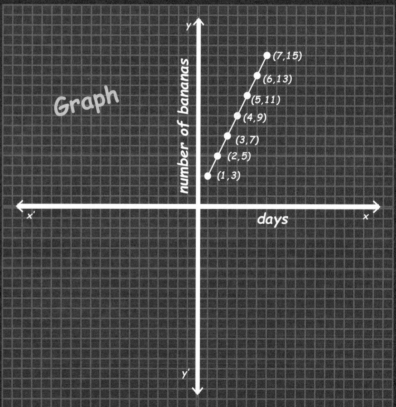

"Equals to" versus "Tends to"

Suppose x is a variable. In a certain condition, x is equal to 2. There is no problem to understand this statement because it is clearly said that x is not greater or less than 2, but exactly 2 at that condition.

But what is the meaning of the following statement?

> 'x tends to 2'

It means x is not equal to exactly 2, but very close to 2. In this case, x may have values, 1.99, 1.999, 2.01, 2.001, 2.0001, 1.999999, but not 2.

=

This is the sign of 'equal to'

→

This is the sign of 'tends to'

Rewrite the following using → (tends to) sign.

- x = 1.00007   Answer x → 1

- x = 3.999999999   Answer x → 4

- x = 5.000000005   Answer x → 5

- x = 7.99999999   Answer x → 8

Suppose you want to calculate the value of, $\dfrac{0}{0}$

It is impossible to calculate because you can not divide any quantity by 0. The result will be undefined.
But if you want to calculate the value of,
$$\frac{0.00008}{0.00002}$$
You should get a finite value, and in the present situation the answer is 4.

Thus we see when the numerator and the denominator both are equal to 0, the result is infinite. But when the numerator and the denominator tend to 0, we should get a finite result.

Now we are going to understand the concept of Limit.

Let's consider a function of x,

$$f(x) = 2x + 1$$

What is the limit of this function at $x \to 0$

Answer:

$$\underset{x \to 0}{\text{Lim}} \ f(x)$$

$$= \underset{x \to 0}{\text{Lim}} \ (2x + 1)$$

$$= (2 \times 0 + 1) \quad \text{[x is replaced by 0 as } x \to 0]$$

$$= 1$$

Thus we can alternatively say that f(x) tends to 1 when x tends to 0.

Now let's take the example of another function,

$$f(x) = \frac{x^2 + 2x}{x}$$

Find the limit of the function when x tends to 0.

Answer:

> If we wanted to find the value of the function when x = 0, we would get,
>
> $$\frac{x^2 + 2x}{x} = \frac{0^2 + 2\times0}{0} = \frac{0}{0}$$
>
> 0/0 is a undefined quantity, so the function is invalid when x is equal to 0.

At $x \longrightarrow 0$,

$$\underset{x \longrightarrow 0}{\text{Lim}} f(x) = \underset{x \longrightarrow 0}{\text{Lim}} \frac{x^2 + 2x}{x}$$

$$= \underset{x \longrightarrow 0}{\text{Lim}} \frac{x(x + 2)}{x}$$

Since $x \neq 0$, we can remove x from the numerator and the denominator.

$$= \underset{x \longrightarrow 0}{\text{Lim}} (x + 2)$$

$$= (0 + 2) = 2$$

...

A function f(x) is said to be continuous at x = a (where a is any numerical value of the variable x) when the values of f(x) at x = a and at x → a are equal.

It can be written mathematically as,

f(x) is continuous at x = a if

$$\lim_{x \to 0} f(x) = f(a)$$

Is the function (2x + 5) continuous at x = 5?

Answer:

$$\lim_{x \to 0} (2x + 5)$$

$$= 2 \times 5 + 5 = 15$$

and,

$$f(5) = 2 \times 5 + 5 = 15$$

Since the function 2x + 5 shows equal values at x = 5 and at x → 5, the function is continuous at x = 5.

Is the function

$$f(x) = \frac{x^2 + x}{x}$$

continuous at x = 0?

Answer:

$$\lim_{x \to 0} \frac{x^2 + x}{x} = \lim_{x \to 0} \frac{x(x + 1)}{x}$$

$$= \lim_{x \to 0} (x + 1)$$

$$= (0 + 1) = 1$$

And, $f(x) = \dfrac{0^2 + 0}{0} = \dfrac{0}{0}$ (Undefined)

Since the values of f(x) are different at x = 0 and x → 0, the function is not continuous at x = 0.

28

OTHER BOOKS BY JOLPIC KIDZ

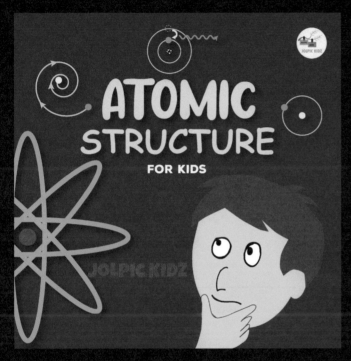

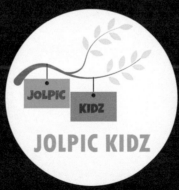

We apply the method of Differentiation to determine the rate of an occurrence.

Suppose the distance of a playground from your home is 60 meter. You take exactly one minute to go there. To estimate how fast or how slow you reach the ground, you need to calculate your walking speed.

Assume that your speed is uniform during your movement. It means you travel equal amount of distance in every second. So to know your speed, you have to calculate the following expression,

$$\text{Speed} = \frac{\text{Distance}}{\text{Time}}$$

Speed is defined as amount of distance traveled in unit time. So your speed is,

$$\frac{60 \text{ meter}}{60 \text{ second}} = 1 \text{ meter/second}$$

If you plot distance versus time in a Cartesian coordinate, you will get the following graph,

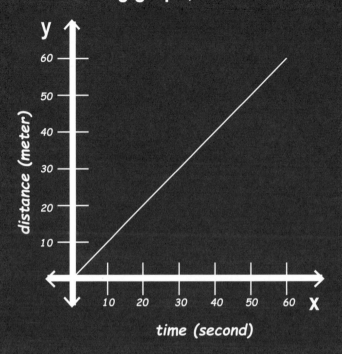

The plot is a straight line which indicates your speed is uniform.

But how would you calculate your speed if your speed was not uniform? In such case, you would get a curved line instead of a straight line just like the below figure.

In this case, you are not able to calculate the speed in a straightforward way. Since your speed varies with time, you are able to calculate it for a certain moment.

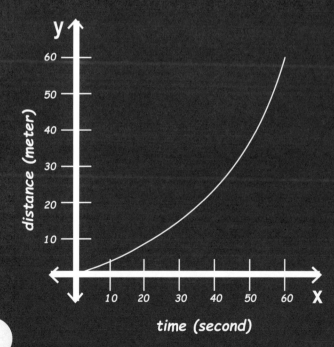

Suppose you want to calculate your speed at 30th second.
    First you have to consider an infinitesimal (a very small quantity which tends to 0) amount of time at 30 second.
    We denote this amount of time by the notation Δt

$$\Delta t \to 0$$

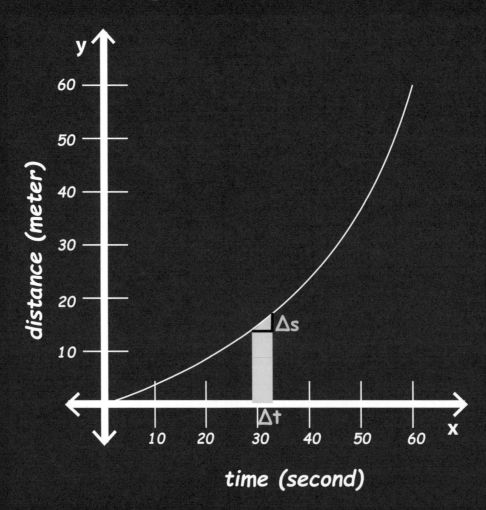

Then you have to consider the amount of distance that you have traveled between 30 second and (30 + Δt) second. Say, that amount of distance is Δs.

Δs is also an infinitesimal quantity.

$$\Delta s \rightarrow 0$$

Thus your speed at 30 second is,

$$\text{Speed} = \frac{\text{Distance}}{\text{Time}} = \frac{\Delta s}{\Delta t}$$

We can alternatively write the following expression

$$\lim_{\substack{\Delta s \rightarrow 0 \\ \Delta t \rightarrow 0}} \frac{\Delta s}{\Delta t} \quad \text{as} \quad \frac{ds}{dt}$$

THIS IS THE BASIC CONCEPT OF

DIFFERENTIATION

Now we are going to understand the concept of differentiation with the help of a few mathematical examples.

In the previous example we considered that you needed 60 seconds to go to the play ground. Suppose your speed is not uniform and your traveled distance is a function of time.

$$f(t) = \frac{t^2}{60}$$

Can you calculate your speed at 30 second?

What is your speed at the moment when you just reach the playground?

Answer:

If we want to calculate the speed at a specific time t, first we have to calculate the traveled distance between the time t and $(t + \Delta t)$.
Since the traveled distance is a function of time, we can calculate it easily.

Total distance traveled in time t is $t^2/60$.
Total distance traveled in time $(t + \Delta t)$ is $(t + \Delta t)^2/60$.

Thus the amount of distance you traveled at the infinitesimal time segment Δt is,

$$(t + \Delta t)^2/60 - t^2/60$$

$$\Delta s = \frac{(t + \Delta t)^2}{60} - \frac{t^2}{60}$$

$$= \frac{t^2 + 2t\Delta t + \Delta t^2}{60} - \frac{t^2}{60}$$

$$= \frac{t^2 + 2t\Delta t + \Delta t^2 - t^2}{60}$$

$$= \frac{2t\Delta t + \Delta t^2}{60}$$

So your speed at time t is,

$$\lim_{\Delta t \to 0} \frac{\Delta s}{\Delta t} = \frac{(2t\Delta t + \Delta t^2)/60}{\Delta t}$$

$$= \frac{t}{30}$$

Δt^2 is neglected because it is a very small quantity

Thus your speed at 30 second is 30/30 = 1 meter/second and you reach the playground at 60 second, then your speed is 60/30 = 2 meter/second.

If we need to determine the rate of change of a function f(x) with respect to the variable x, we should apply the method of differentiation.

Mathematically it is expressed as,

$$\frac{d}{dx} f(x) = \lim_{\Delta x \to 0} \frac{f(x + \Delta x) - f(x)}{\Delta x}$$

Suppose a body is moving with displacement $(t + t^2)$ meter. Determine the speed at 20 second. (Here t represents the variable, time)

Answer:

Here the function is,

$$f(t) = t + t^2$$

Thus,

$$\frac{d}{dx} f(t) = \lim_{\Delta t \to 0} \frac{f(t + \Delta t) - f(t)}{\Delta t}$$

$$\frac{d}{dx} f(t) = \underset{\Delta t \to 0}{\text{Lim}} \frac{[(t + \Delta t) + (t + \Delta t)^2] - [t + t^2]}{\Delta t}$$

$$= \underset{\Delta t \to 0}{\text{Lim}} \frac{\Delta t(1 + 2t)}{\Delta t}$$

Simplifying the numerator

$$= 1 + 2t$$

The speed of the body at time t second is (1 + 2t) meter. So at 20 second, the speed is (1 + 2×20) = 41 meter.

∫ INTEGRATION

The term Integration has the reverse meaning of Differentiation.

If differentiation of a function f(x) with respect to x yields a new function g(x),

$$\frac{d}{dx} f(x) = g(x)$$

According to the definition of Integration, we can write,

$$\int g(x)\ dx = f(x) + C$$

Where C is any constant

We go back to the previous example to understand the meaning of Integration.

Previously the function $f(t) = t + t^2$ were given representing the displacement of a body, and determined the speed differentiating the function.

$$\frac{d}{dx} (t + t^2) = 1 + 2t$$

Now the problem is given reverse.

A body is moving with speed $(1 + 2t)$ meter/sec. Calculate its displacement during 4th to 10th second.

Here we are going to apply Integration to find the answer

$$\int_{4}^{10} (1 + 2t) \, dt = [t + t^2]_{4}^{10}$$

$$= [10 + 10^2] - [4 + 4^2]$$

$$= 110 - 20 = 90$$

Thus its displacement during 4th to 10th second is 90 meter.

The Concept of Integration on Cartesian Coordinate

Suppose a function Y = f(x) is represented by the following curve.

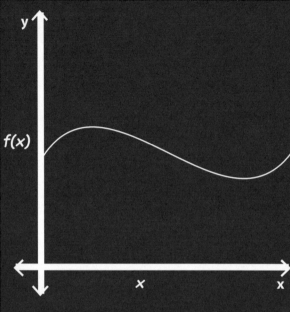

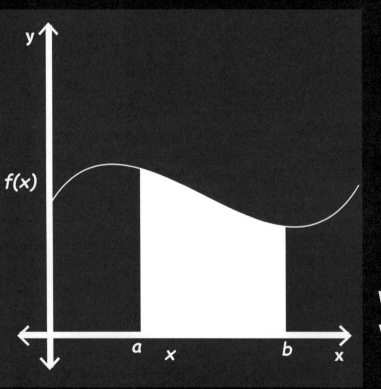

The area of the shaded region under the curve is,

$$\int_a^b f(x)\ dx$$

Where b and a are two numerical values of the variable x.

Let's understand the meaning of

$$\int_a^b f(x) \, dx$$

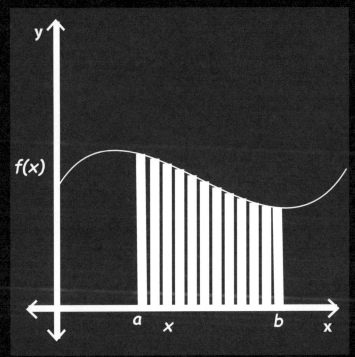

First divide the shaded region into several vertical segments. Each segment is a rectangle with infinitesimally narrow width Δx, and its height has the value of f(x) at the respective value of x. For example, at x = a, the height of the rectangle is f(a) and its width is Δx.

So the area of that infinitesimally narrow rectangle is,

$$f(a) \times \Delta x$$

To evaluate the total area, we should add the areas of all individual rectangles,

$$\underset{\Delta x \to 0}{\text{Lim}} \; f(a) \times \Delta x + f(a_1) \times \Delta x + f(a_2) \times \Delta x + f(a_3) \times \Delta x + \ldots\ldots + f(b) \times \Delta x$$

$$= \underset{\Delta x \to 0}{\text{Lim}} \sum_{x=a}^{b} f(x) \times \Delta x \quad = \quad \int_a^b f(x) \, dx$$

This is the geometrical meaning of Integration.

THE END